3 1526 04140974 6

PIANO . VOCAL . GUITAR

the music glee

The Christmas Album

ISBN 978-1-4584-0819-8

HAL•LEONARD® CORPORATION

7777 W. BLUEMOUND RD. P.O. BOX 13819 MILWAUKEE, WI 53213

Visit Hal Leonard Online at
www.halleonard.com

WE NEED A LITTLE CHRISTMAS

Music and Lyric by
JERRY HERMAN

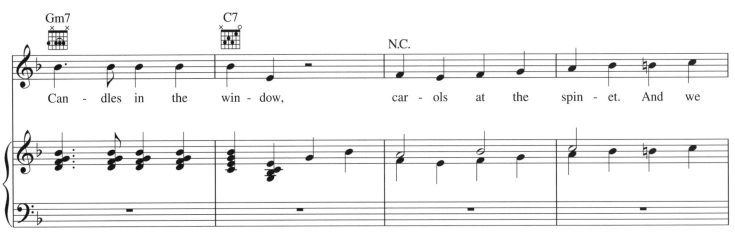

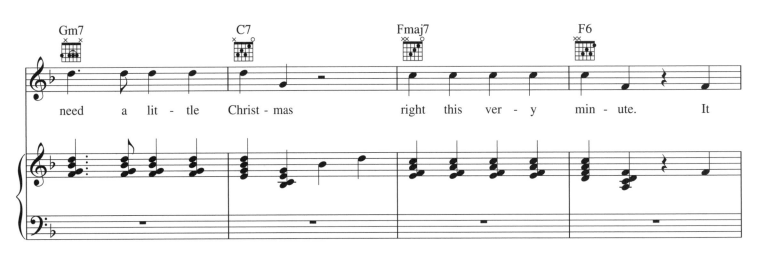

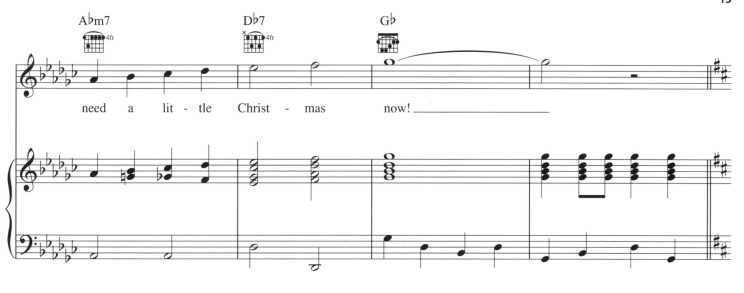

need   a   lit - tle   Christ - mas   now! _____

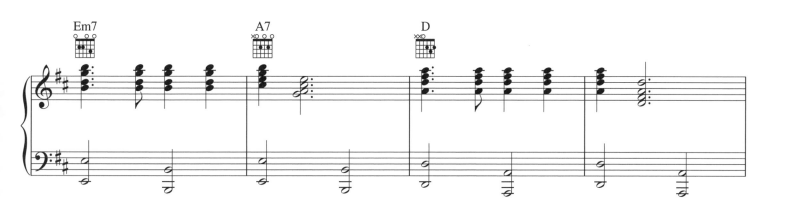

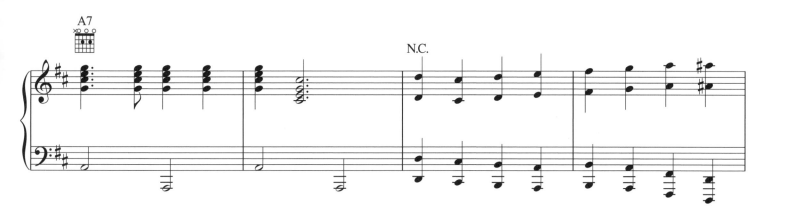

DECK THE ROOFTOP

Words and Music by ADAM ANDERS,
PEER ASTROM and NIKKI HASSMAN

Fa la la la, oh ____ oh, fa la la la,

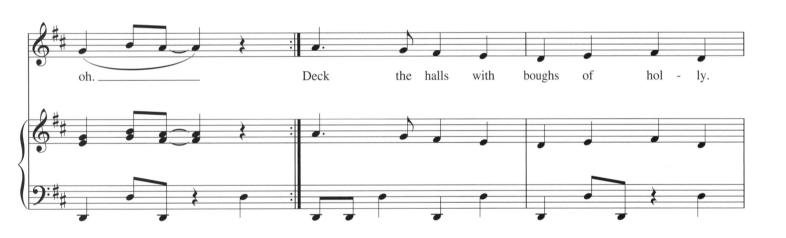

oh. ____ Deck the halls with boughs of hol-ly.

fa la la la la la la la la. 'Tis the sea-son

click   click   click,   down through the chim - ney with   good   Saint   Nick.

Deck   the halls,   he's   up   on   the   roof - top.   Deck   the   halls,   he's

up   on   the   roof - top.   Deck   the   halls,   he's   up   on   the   roof - top.

Fa   la   la   la.   Fa   la   la   la.   First   comes   the   stock - ing   of

22

MERRY CHRISTMAS, DARLING

Words and Music by RICHARD CARPENTER
and FRANK POOLER

BABY, IT'S COLD OUTSIDE

By FRANK LOESSER

THE MOST WONDERFUL DAY OF THE YEAR

Music and Lyrics by
JOHNNY MARKS

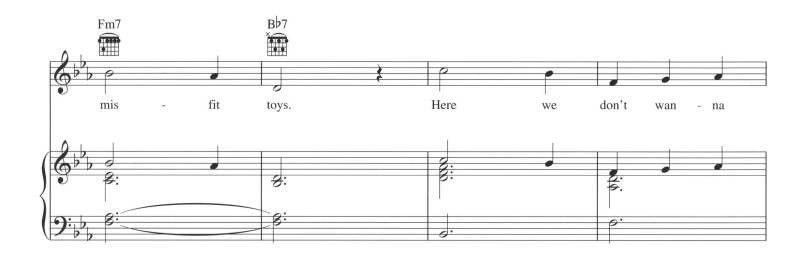

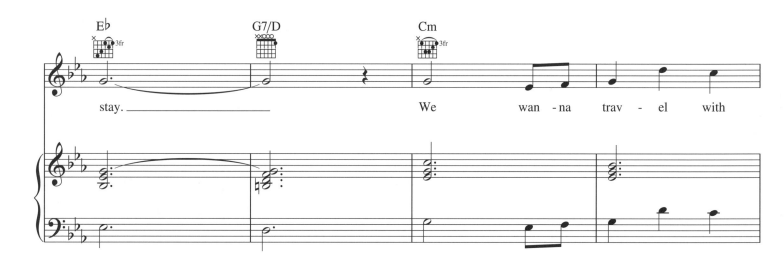

LAST CHRISTMAS

Words and Music by
GEORGE MICHAEL

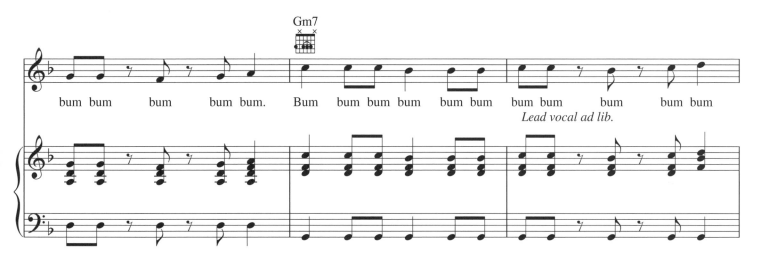

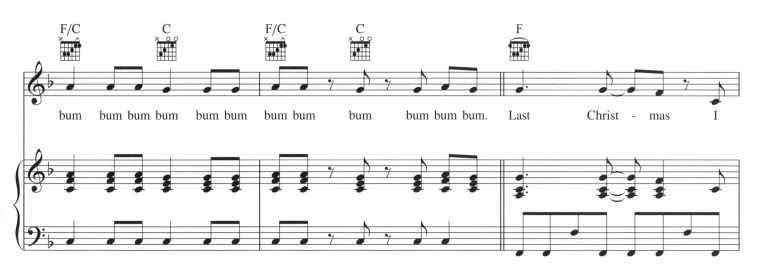

GOD REST YE MERRY, GENTLEMEN

19th Century English Carol
Arranged by ADAM ANDERS,
PEER ASTROM and NIKKI HASSMAN

Moderately

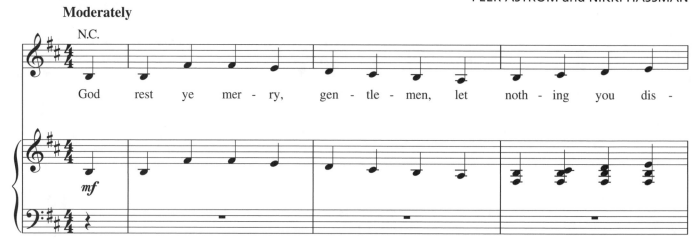

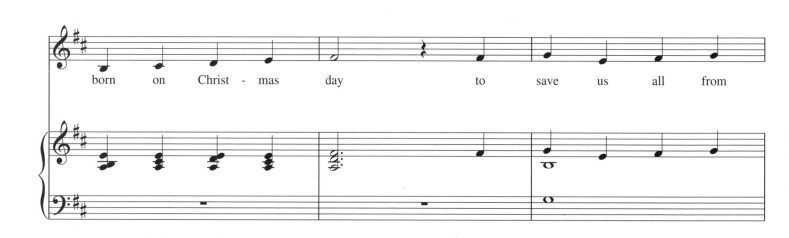

50

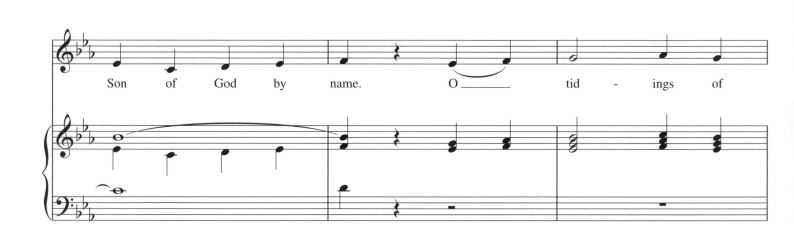

52

54

O CHRISTMAS TREE

Traditional German Carol
Arranged by ADAM ANDERS
and PEER ASTROM

JINGLE BELLS

Words and Music by J. PIERPONT
Arranged by ADAM ANDERS
and PEER ASTROM

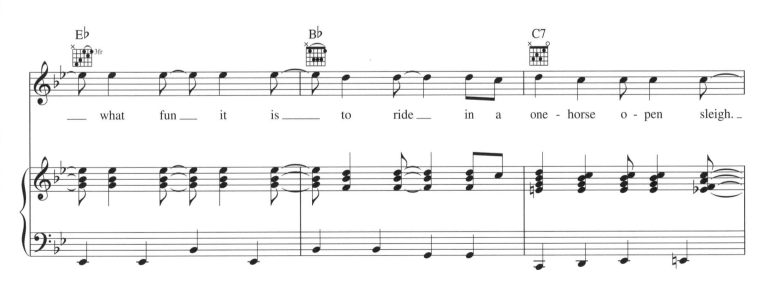

YOU'RE A MEAN ONE, MISTER GRINCH

Lyrics by DR. SEUSS
Music by ALBERT HAGUE

* Recorded a half step higher.

ANGELS WE HAVE HEARD ON HIGH

Traditional French Carol
Translated by JAMES CHADWICK
Arranged by ADAM ANDERS and PEER ASTROM

O HOLY NIGHT

French Words by PLACIDE CAPPEAU
English Words by JOHN S. DWIGHT
Music by ADOLPHE ADAM
Arranged by ADAM ANDERS
and PEER ASTROM